Introduction

When I started freesciencelessons in 2013, I had one simple goal[ ] their understanding of science. When I was at school (and we're ta[ ] now), science was always my favourite subject. It's not surprising that I went on to become a science teacher. I know that many students find science challenging. But I really believe that this doesn't have to be the case. With patient teaching and a bit of hard work, any student can make amazing progress.

Back in 2013, I had no idea how big freesciencelessons would become. The channel now has nearly 70 million views from 192 countries with a total view time of over 300 years. I love to hear from the students who have patiently watched the videos and realised that they can do science after all, despite in many cases having little confidence in their ability. And just like in 2013, I still make all the videos myself (many students think that I have a staff of helpers, but no, it's just me).

This workbook is designed to complement the Biology 2 videos for the AQA specification. However, there is a huge amount of overlap with other exam boards and in the future I'll be making videos and workbooks for those as well. I've packed the workbook full of questions to help you with your science learning. You might decide to start at the beginning and answer every question in the book or you might prefer to dip in and out of chapters depending on what you want to learn. Either way is fine. I've also written very detailed answers for every question, again to help you really develop your understanding. You can find these by scanning the QR code on the front of the book or by visiting freesciencelessons.co.uk/b2cshv1

Please don't think of science as some sort of impossible mountain to climb. Yes there are some challenging bits but it's not as difficult as people think. Take your time, work hard and believe in yourself. When you find a topic difficult, don't give up. Just go to a different topic and come back to it later.

Finally, if you have any feedback on the workbooks, you're welcome to let me know (support@freesciencelessons.co.uk). I'm always keen to make the workbooks better so if you have a suggestion, I'd love to hear it.

Good luck on your journey. I hope that you get the grades that you want.

Shaun Donnelly

Revision Tips

The first important point about revision is that you need to be realistic about the amount of work that you need to do. Essentially you have to learn two years of work (or three if you start GCSEs in Year 9). That's a lot of stuff to learn. So give yourself plenty of time. If you're very serious about getting a top grade then I would recommend starting your revision as early as you can. I see a lot of messages on Youtube and Twitter from students who leave their revision until the last minute. That's their choice but I don't think it's a good way to get the best grades.

To revise successfully for any subject (but I believe particularly for science), you have to really get into it. You have to get your mind deep into the subject. That's because science has some difficult concepts that require thought and concentration. So you're right in the middle of that challenging topic and your phone pings. Your friend has sent you a message about something that he saw on Netflix. You reply and start revising again. Another message appears. This is from a different friend who has a meme they want to share. And so on and so on.

What I'm trying to tell you is that successful revision requires isolation. You need to shut yourself away from distractions and that includes your phone. Nothing that any of your friends have to say is so critically important that it cannot wait until you have finished. Just because your friends are bored does not mean that your revision has to suffer. Again, it's about you taking control.

Remember to give yourself breaks every now and then. You'll know when it's time. I don't agree with people who say you need a break every fifteen minutes (or whatever). Everyone is different and you might find that your work is going so well that you don't need a break. In that case don't take one. If you're taking breaks every ten minutes then the question I would ask is do you need them? Or are you trying to avoid work?

There are many different ways to revise and you have to find what works for you. I believe that active revision is the most effective. I know that many students like to copy out detailed notes (often from my videos). Personally, I don't believe that this is a great way to revise since it's not really active. A better way is to watch a video and then try to answer the questions from this book. If you can't, then you might want to watch the video again (or look carefully at the answers to check the part that you struggled with).

The human brain learns by repetition. So the more times that you go over a concept, the more fixed it will become in your brain. That's why revision needs so much time because you really need to go over everything more than once (ideally several times) before the exam.

Revision Tips

I find with my students that flashcards are a great way to learn facts. Again, that's because the brain learns by repetition. My students write a question on one side and the answer on the other. They then practise them until they've memorised the answer. I always advise them to start by memorising five cards and then gradually adding in extra cards, rather than try to memorise fifty cards at once.

I've noticed over the last few years that more students do past paper practise as a way of revising. I do not recommend this at all. A past paper is what you do AFTER you have revised. Imagine that you are trying to learn to play the guitar. So you buy a guitar and rather than having lessons, you book yourself into a concert hall to give a performance. And you keep giving performances until you can play. Would you recommend that as a good strategy? I wouldn't. But essentially that's how lots of students try to revise. Yes by all means do practise papers (I've included a specimen paper in this book for you) but do them at the end when you've done all your revision. Past papers require you to pull lots of different bits of the specification together, so you should only do them when you are capable of that (ie when you've already done loads of revision).

A couple of final points ....

To reduce our environmental impact and to keep the price of this book reasonable, the answers are available online. Simply scan the QR code on the front or visit www.freesciencelessons.co.uk/b2cshv1

There will be times when I decide to update a book, for example to make something clearer or maybe to correct a problem (I hope not many of those). So please keep an eye out for updates. I'll post them on Twitter (@UKscienceguy) and also on the FAQ page of my website. If you think that you've spotted a mistake or a problem, please feel free to contact me.

Copyright information: The copyright of this workbook belongs to Shaun Donnelly. Copying of this workbook is strictly prohibited. Anyone found in breach of copyright will be prosecuted.

Contents

Contents

Contents

Contents

Chapter 1: Homeostasis

- Describe what is meant by homeostasis and why this is essential for animals.
- Describe the different parts and functions of a homeostatic control system.
- Describe what is meant by the central nervous system and the stages of a reflex arc.
- Describe how to investigate the factors that affect reaction time (required practical).
- Name the main glands in the endocrine system and state their functions.
- Describe how the blood glucose concentration is regulated by the pancreas.
- Describe type 1 and type 2 diabetes and how these are managed.
- Describe the roles of hormones in the menstrual cycle.
- Compare the advantages and disadvantages of the different methods of contraception.
- Describe how hormones can be used to treat infertility including the stages of in vitro fertilisation (IVF).
- Describe the issues around IVF including ethical considerations.
- Describe the role of the adrenal glands.
- Describe what is meant by negative feedback and give examples of negative feedback systems.

Homeostasis

1. Homeostasis is essential for animals to function effectively.

a. Complete the sentences below by using the correct words from the list.

homeostasis   **internal**   **stable**   **enzymes**   **external**   **respiration**

Every reaction in a cell is catalysed by _____ . A good example is _____

which releases energy from glucose. Enzymes need _____ conditions to work effectively.

These conditions are maintained by _____ . Homeostasis is defined as the regulation of

the _____ conditions of a cell or organism to maintain optimal conditions for function in

response to internal and _____ changes.

b. Connect the correct boxes below to show how the body's internal conditions change due to intense exercise.

Blood glucose levels	Increase	Sweating releases water to cool the body down
Body temperature	Decrease	More glucose is used to release energy by respiration
Blood water levels	Decrease	Increased respiration releases more thermal energy

2. The diagram shows the general features of a homeostatic control system.

a. Receptor cells detect a stimulus (ie a change to the body's internal or external environment).

Give an example of a change to the body's internal and external environment.

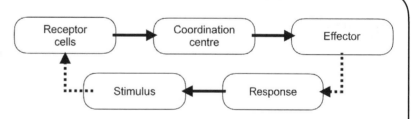

b. Receptor cells pass the information to the coordination centre eg the spinal cord or pancreas.

Describe the function of the coordination centre.

c. The coordination centre passes instructions to the effectors.

State two examples of effectors.

d. Describe the role of effectors in homeostasis.

The Nervous System

Exam tip: We looked at the structure of neurones in the Biology 1 video Animal Cell Specialisation. I would recommend that you rewatch that video before attempting this section.

1. The diagram shows the overall structure of the human nervous system.

a. Label the diagram to show the two parts of the central nervous system.

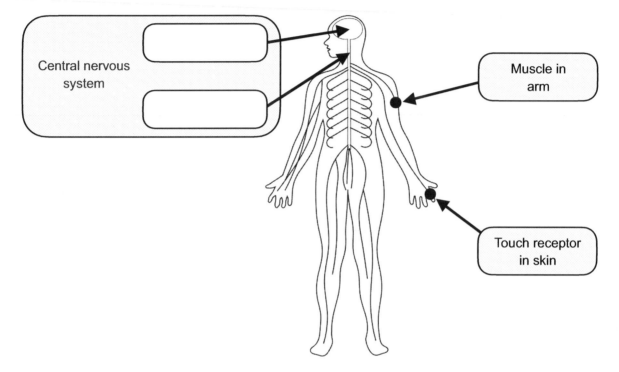

Central nervous system

Muscle in arm

Touch receptor in skin

b. The diagram also shows neurones running to and from the central nervous system.

Circle the correct words to show the functions of these neurones.

A stimulus is detected by receptors / effectors. These send chemical signals / electrical impulses down neurones to the central nervous system.

The central nervous system acts as the coordination centre. Chemical signals / electrical impulses now pass from the central nervous system to the receptors / effectors which bring about a response.

c. The diagram shows a receptor and an effector. Label the attached neurones to show the direction of the electrical impulses in each case.

d. Effectors are normally muscles or glands. Describe what muscles and glands do to bring about a response.

Muscles

Glands

2. Reflexes are fast, automatic responses often to a threat or danger.

The diagram below shows the pathway of a reflex.

Label the diagram using the labels below.

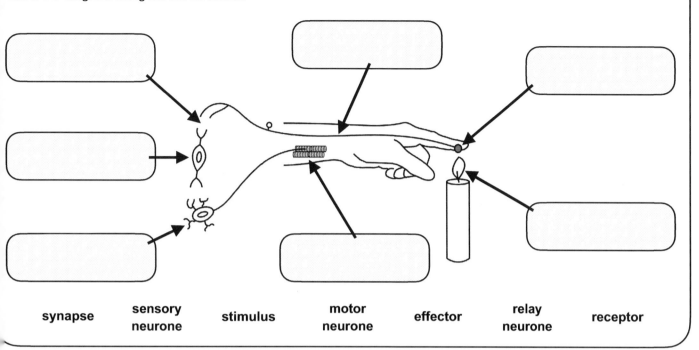

| synapse | sensory neurone | stimulus | motor neurone | effector | relay neurone | receptor |

3. The boxes below show the stages of the reflex arc.

a. Number the boxes to show the correct order.

| The muscle contracts and the hand pulls away (the response) | The electrical impulses reach the synapse at the end of the sensory neurone | An electrical impulse is triggered in the relay neurone |

| A chemical is released at the synapse | **6** The chemical diffuses to the relay neurone | At the next synapse a chemical is released |

| Electrical impulses are triggered in the motor neurone | Electrical impulses pass down the sensory neurone | The electrical impulses travel towards the central nervous system |

1 The stimulus (heat) is detected by receptors in the skin | The impulses reach the effector (a muscle) | **10** The impulses travel away from the central nervous system |

b. Which of the neurones in the reflex arc are in the central nervous system?

| sensory neurone | motor neurone | relay neurone |

c. Explain why reflexes are automatic and rapid.

Required Practical: Reaction Time

1. In this practical, we investigate the factors that can affect a person's reaction time.

a. First, person 1 sits at a table. Person 1 should have good upright posture.

Why do you think that this posture is better than a slouched, comfortable posture?

b. Person 1 now places their dominant arm on the table so their dominant hand is over the edge.

What is meant by their dominant hand?

c. Person 2 holds a metre ruler vertically so the zero cm mark is between person 1's thumb and index finger.

Why is it important that this position does not change?

d. Person 2 now tells person 1 to prepare. Person 2 then drops the ruler at a random time and person 1 has to catch the ruler as quickly as possible.

Person 2 now records the measurement on the ruler that is level with the top of person 1's thumb.

Why is it important that the measurement is always at the top of person 1's thumb?

e. Person 1 has a short rest and then the test is repeated several times. A mean value is taken of the results and person 1's reaction time is determined using a table.

At this point, person 1 and 2 switch places and person 2's reaction time is determined.

What are the independent variable and dependent variable in this experiment?

f. Control variables are kept the same throughout the experiment.

State the control variables and explain why it is important that we keep these the same.

2. Two other independent variables that we could investigate are shown below.

Describe how we would carry out these experiments and the results we would expect to see.

The effect of practise

Dominant versus non-dominant hand

3. We could also investigate the effect of drinking caffeine on a person's reaction time. Caffeine is a stimulant.

To do this, we measure the reaction time of a volunteer before and after drinking cola.

a. In this experiment, we also need to measure the person's reaction time after drinking caffeine-free cola.

Explain why this is important.

b. Describe two ways that we can make the experiment safe.

The table shows a person's reaction times in this experiment.

c. Plot these results on the bar chart below.

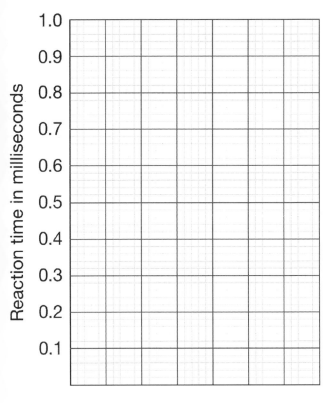

Condition

Reaction time in milliseconds		
Before drinking	After drinking caffeine-free cola	After drinking cola with caffeine
0.8	0.6	0.3

d. What do these results show about the effect of drinking caffeine on reaction time?

e. Suggest why the student's reaction time decreased after drinking caffeine-free cola.

The Endocrine System

1. The endocrine system produces a large number of effects in the human body.

a. Complete the sentences below by circling the correct words.

The endocrine system consists of a number of

| organs |
| glands |
| nerves |

. These secrete chemicals called

| enzymes |
| cells |
| hormones |

directly into the

| blood |
| saliva |
| urine |

. These travel around the body but only produce an effect in

| target organs |
| the digestive system |
| the nervous system |

b. Write "N" if the statements below apply to the nervous system and "E" if they apply to the endocrine system.

| This produces a slower, longer lasting effect | Electrical impulses are transmitted along neurones | Chemicals called hormones are carried in the bloodstream | This produces a very rapid, short-lived effect |

2. The glands in the endocrine system are shown below.

a. Label each gland and then draw lines to link the glands with the correct function.

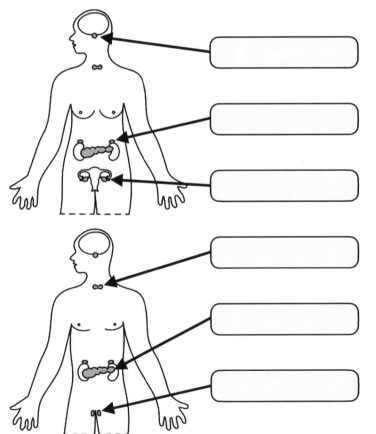

Release adrenaline in response to fear and stress

Control puberty and reproduction in females

Controls the concentration of glucose in the bloodstream

Releases hormones which control other endocrine glands

Controls growth and the body's basal metabolic rate

Control puberty and reproduction in males

b. Explain why the pituitary gland is called the "master gland".

Control of Blood Glucose

1. The control of blood glucose is a critical part of homeostasis.

a. Explain why it is so important that the blood glucose concentration is controlled.

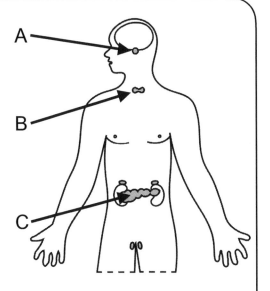

b. The blood glucose concentration is controlled by the pancreas.

Circle the letter below which shows the pancreas.

c. The diagram shows how the pancreas regulates the concentration of glucose in the blood.

Complete the flow charts by deleting the incorrect words.

After a meal rich in carbohydrates	**In between meals**
Blood glucose concentration increases / decreases	Blood glucose concentration increases / decreases
The rise / fall in blood glucose is sensed by the pancreas	The rise / fall in blood glucose is sensed by the pancreas
The pancreas secretes insulin / glucagon into the bloodstream	The pancreas secretes insulin / glucagon into the bloodstream
Insulin triggers cells to absorb / release glucose from / into the blood	Glucagon triggers liver cells to convert glycogen / starch to glucose
Muscle and liver cells store excess glucose as glycogen / starch	Glucose is released into the digestive system / bloodstream
Blood glucose concentration rises / falls back to its normal level	Blood glucose concentration rises / falls back to its normal level

2. The graph shows how a person's blood glucose concentration changes throughout the day.

a. Write "I" to show when insulin is released by the pancreas and "G" to show when glucagon is released.

b. Insulin and glucagon have opposite effects on blood glucose concentration.

What name do scientists give to systems like this?

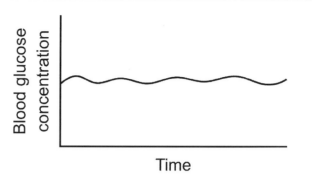

3. People with diabetes cannot control their blood glucose effectively.

a. How is a person with type 1 diabetes different from a person without diabetes?

b. The graph shows the changes in blood glucose concentration in a person with type 1 diabetes and a person without diabetes.

Both people were given the same amount of glucose at the start of the experiment.

Describe two differences in how the blood glucose concentration changes between the two people.

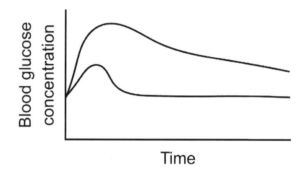

c. How do people with type 1 diabetes manage their blood glucose concentration?

4. In the UK, many people now have type 2 diabetes.

a. Explain how the control of blood glucose is not working in type 2 diabetes.

b. Describe how type 2 diabetes is managed.

c. Suggest why the incidence of type 2 diabetes is increasing in the UK.

The Menstrual Cycle

1. Hormones control the onset of puberty in both males and females.

This involves the development of secondary sex characteristics such as pubic hair.

Complete the boxes to show where testosterone and oestrogen are produced.

Males

The _____ make testosterone
which triggers sperm formation.

Females

The _____ make oestrogen
which triggers the menstrual cycle.

2. The diagram below shows the approximate timings of the menstrual cycle.

Use the labels below to describe what is happening at each stage.

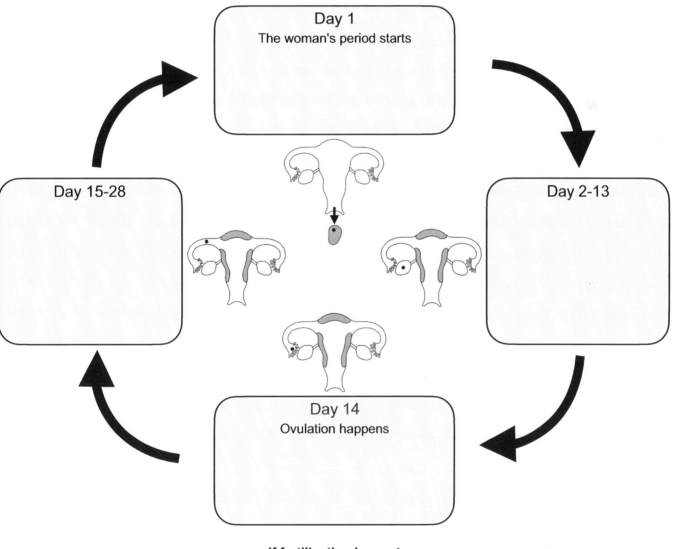

Day 1
The woman's period starts

Day 15-28

Day 2-13

Day 14
Ovulation happens

A mature egg
is released
from the ovary

If fertilisation has not
happened, the uterus lining and
unfertilised egg are released

The uterus
lining starts to
thicken

An egg matures
in an ovary

If the egg is
fertilised, it implants
into the uterus wall

The egg makes
its way down a
fallopian tube

3. Draw lines to link the correct hormone in the menstrual cycle to the correct function.

| Oestrogen | | This is produced by the ovary and keeps the uterus lining thick incase a fertilised egg implants |

| Follicle-stimulating hormone (FSH) | | This is produced by the pituitary gland and causes an egg to be released by the ovary (ovulation) |

| Luteinising hormone (LH) | | This is produced by the ovaries and causes the uterus lining to thicken ready for a fertilised egg to implant |

| Progesterone | | This is produced by the pituitary gland and causes an egg to mature in an ovary |

4. Using the words below, complete the boxes to describe the menstrual cycle.

First the _____ gland releases FSH into the bloodstream.

The FSH travels to the _____ and causes an egg to mature.

FSH also triggers the release of the hormone _____ by the ovaries.

Oestrogen causes the lining of the _____ to become thick.

Oestrogen also _____ the pituitary gland releasing FSH.

Oestrogen now triggers the pituitary gland to release_____ .

LH triggers the ovary to release the mature egg (_____).

ovulation   LH   uterus   ovaries   oestrogen   pituitary   prevents

At this point the ovary releases the hormone_____ .

Progesterone stops the pituitary gland releasing FSH and_____ .

Progesterone also makes sure that the uterus lining stays_____ .

If the egg is not _____ then progesterone levels fall.

The uterus lining and egg are released. The woman has her_____ .

fertilised   period   LH   progesterone   thickened

5. The graph below shows how the levels of hormones change during the menstrual cycle.

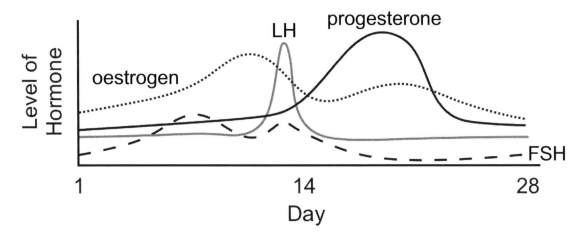

a. The pituitary gland releases FSH which triggers an egg to mature in the ovary.

FSH also triggers the ovary to produce oestrogen. Explain how this is supported by the data in the graph.

b. Increasing levels of oestrogen inhibit the production of FSH. Explain how this is supported by the graph.

c. Suggest what would happen in the ovaries if oestrogen did not inhibit the production of FSH.

d. When oestrogen reaches a certain level, this triggers the pituitary gland to release LH.

What is the purpose of the LH?

e. Once the egg has been released, the ovary produces progesterone. What is the role of progesterone?

f. High levels of progesterone prevent the pituitary gland from producing FSH and LH.

Explain why this is important.

g. What do scientists call control systems such as the menstrual cycle?

Contraception

1. Contraception is designed to prevent fertilisation.

a. Hormonal contraceptives include the pill, an implant, an injection and a skin patch.

Describe how hormonal contraceptives prevent a woman from becoming pregnant.

b. The table below describes the advantages and disadvantages of hormonal contraceptives.

Decide whether each statement applies to the contraceptive pill or patches, implants and injections.

Then write "A" for advantages and "D" for disadvantages in the correct boxes below.

	Contraceptive pill	Contraceptive patch, implants and injection
Highly effective if used correctly		
Increased risk of breast cancer or blood clots		Does not apply
Does not protect against sexually transmitted infections (STIs) eg HIV		
Long lasting so convenient	Does not apply	
Must be taken daily to prevent pregnancy		Does not apply

2. Barrier methods of contraception include condoms and the diaphragm.

a. Complete the box below to show how barrier methods work.

Barrier methods prevent fertilisation by _____ the sperm reaching an egg.

Because barrier methods do not use hormones, they have no _____ .

Unlike hormonal contraceptives, barrier methods reduce the risk of _____ .

b. Describe a disadvantage of using condoms as a form of contraception.

c. Condoms and a diaphragm are more effective if used with a spermicide gel.

Describe how a spermicide works.

3. Many women use an intrauterine device (IUD) as a form of contraception.

This is also called the coil.

a. How does an IUD prevent a woman from becoming pregnant? Tick two boxes.

| Prevents ovulation | Stops an egg maturing | Kills sperm | Prevents a fertilised egg implanting in the uterus | Can release hormones to reduce chance of fertilisation |

b. Describe the advantages of an IUD compared to hormonal or barrier methods of contraception.

c. Describe the main disadvantage of using an IUD as a form of contraception compared to barrier methods.

4. Surgical forms of contraception are called sterilisation. Sterilisation is a highly effective form of contraception.

a. Describe how sterilisation works in a man and in a woman.

| Sterilisation in men | Sterilisation in women |

b. Describe two disadvantages of sterilisation.

5. Some people practise natural forms of contraception.

a. Describe how natural contraception works.

b. Complete the box below by circling the correct words.

Natural contraception is   easy / difficult.   This is because it is   easy / difficult   to tell if a

woman has ovulated. Natural contraception   does / does not   protect against STIs.

6. Some people think that contraceptive choices is an ethical issue and cannot be answered by science alone.

Explain what is meant by an ethical issue and give an example.

Hormones to Treat Infertility

1. Hormones can be used to help people who have difficulty conceiving.

a. Complete the sentences below by circling the correct words.

Eggs are triggered to mature in an ovary by the hormone

> oestrogen
> LH
> FSH

. Once the egg has matured it is

released from the ovary. This process is called ovulation and is triggered by the hormone

> FSH
> LH
> oestrogen

.

Both of these hormones are produced by the

> thyroid
> pituitary
> adrenal

gland.

b. Women who have trouble conceiving can be given a "fertility drug".

Describe what is contained in a fertility drug and explain how this can help a woman become pregnant.

2. In vitro fertilisation (IVF) can also be used to help with infertility for example in men with a low sperm count.

a. The boxes below show the stages of IVF. Number the boxes in the correct order.

The eggs are fertilised by the sperm in the lab	The fertilised eggs develop into embryos	The woman is treated with FSH and LH	The embryos develop into babies
The embryos are inserted into the woman's uterus	The eggs are collected from the mother	Several eggs mature in an ovary	Sperm is collected from the father

b. Although IVF allows a couple to have a baby of their own, it does have problems.

Complete the sentences below by selecting the correct words from the list.

multiple   **several**   **success**   **emotionally**   **demanding**

IVF is _____ stressful for both parents and physically _____ for the mother.

There is a risk of _____ births which is very risky for both the mother and the babies.

IVF also has a low _____ rate and often requires _____ attempts.

c. Describe two ethical issues around IVF.

Negative Feedback

1. Adrenaline is a hormone produced by the adrenal glands during fear or stress.

a. Label the diagram to show the adrenal glands.

b. Describe the effect of adrenaline on the heart.

c. Explain how this prepares the body to fight or to run away.

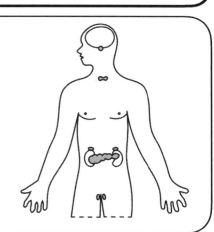

2. Many hormones in the endocrine system are regulated by negative feedback.

A good example is thyroxine.

a. Thyroxine is produced by the thyroid gland. Label this on the diagram.

b. The basal metabolic rate is how fast the chemical reactions in the body take place.

Describe the effect of thyroxine on the basal metabolic rate.

c. Describe another process which is regulated by thyroxine.

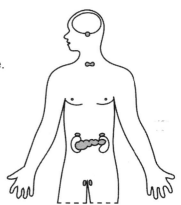

d. The diagrams show how thyroxine levels are regulated by negative feedback.

Complete the boxes using the correct descriptions below.

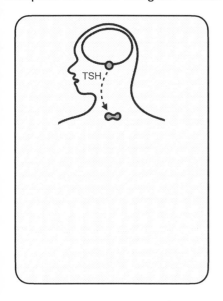
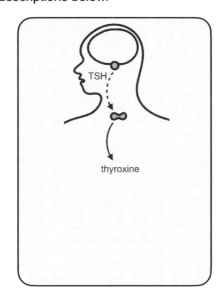
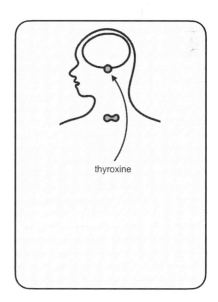

Increasing thyroxine levels are sensed by the brain	**Thyroxine levels fall too low**	**Thyroid gland produces less thyroxine**
TSH triggers thyroid gland to produce more thyroxine	**Pituitary gland stops releasing TSH**	**Pituitary gland releases TSH into blood**

e. State two other systems which are regulated by negative feedback.

Chapter 2 : Inheritance

- Describe what is meant by a gamete and how gametes are different to normal body cells in terms of the number of chromosomes.

- Describe the differences between sexual reproduction and asexual reproduction.

- Describe the stages in meiosis and how this leads to the formation of gametes.

- Describe what is meant by fertilisation and differentiation.

- Describe what is meant by a gene and the genome.

- Describe the possible benefits of studying the human genome.

- Describe the structure of DNA in terms of the double helix.

- Describe what is meant by an allele and describe the difference between a dominant and a recessive allele.

- Describe how alleles can be homozygous or heterozygous.

- Describe what is meant by genotype and phenotype.

- Construct genetic diagrams showing how cystic fibrosis and polydactyly are inherited.

- Explain how a person can be a carrier of a recessive allele but not a carrier of a dominant allele.

- Interpret family trees to describe how alleles are inherited.

- Describe how sex is inherited in humans.

Sexual and Asexual Reproduction

1. The chromosomes in a cell contain the instructions which the cell uses to carry out its function.

a. Complete the sentences below by using the correct words from the list.

paired   meiosis   copies   identical   gametes   nucleus   pairs

We find chromosomes in the _____ of cells. In a normal human cell, there are 23

_____ of chromosomes. Normal human cells are produced by a type of cell division

called mitosis. Mitosis produces two identical _____ of a cell. However, cells such as

sperm and eggs are different. These are called _____ . In these, the chromosomes

are not _____ . Human gametes contain 23 single chromosomes. Gametes are

formed by a type of cell division called _____ . Gametes are not _____ .

Cell A   Cell B

b. The diagram shows two types of cells.

How does the number of chromosomes show that these cells are not from a human?

c. Tick the correct boxes below to show which statement applies to which cell.

	Cell A	Cell B
This cell was produced by cell division by mitosis	☐	☐
The chromosomes are not paired	☐	☐
The chromosomes are found in pairs	☐	☐
This cell could be a sperm or egg cell	☐	☐
This cell was produced by cell division by meiosis	☐	☐

2. Animals and flowering plants carry out sexual reproduction.

The diagram shows a sperm cell fusing (joining) with an egg cell.

a. State the names of the gametes in flowering plants.

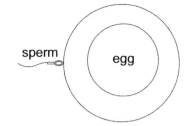

b. Complete the sentences below by circling the correct words.

Sperm, eggs and pollen are all examples of gametes. When gametes join, this is called

| implantation |
| fertilisation |
| reproduction |

.

In sexual reproduction there is a

| mixing |
| splitting |
| separation |

of genetic information from the male and female parents.

There is variation in the offspring because every gamete is genetically

| identical |
| equal |
| different |

to each other.

---

3. The diagram shows a spider plant.

Spider plants can carry out asexual reproduction.

a. The baby spider plants are genetically identical to the parent plant.

What do scientists call genetically identical organisms?

b. Explain why the baby spider plants are genetically identical to the parent spider plant.

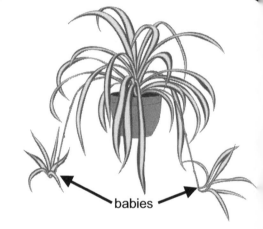

babies

c. The following statements apply to either sexual reproduction or asexual reproduction.

Write "S" next to the statements which apply to sexual reproduction and "AS" next to asexual reproduction.

| Only one parent needed | Only involves mitosis | Involves meiosis |

| Offspring are genetically identical | Involves fertilisation | Does not involve fertilisation | Offspring are not genetically identical |

| Involves gametes | Two parents needed | No gametes used |

Meiosis and Fertilisation

1. Meiosis is essential for sexual reproduction.

a. Circle the boxes below to show where meiosis takes place.

| Cells in the heart | Cells in the testes | Cells in the lungs | Cells in the brain | Cells in the ovaries |

b. Meiosis produces gametes.

Describe the difference between a gamete cell and a normal body cell (eg a muscle cell).

c. The stages of meiosis are shown below.

Remember that normal human cells have 23 chromosome pairs. However, only three chromosome pairs are shown.

Describe what is taking place during each stage.

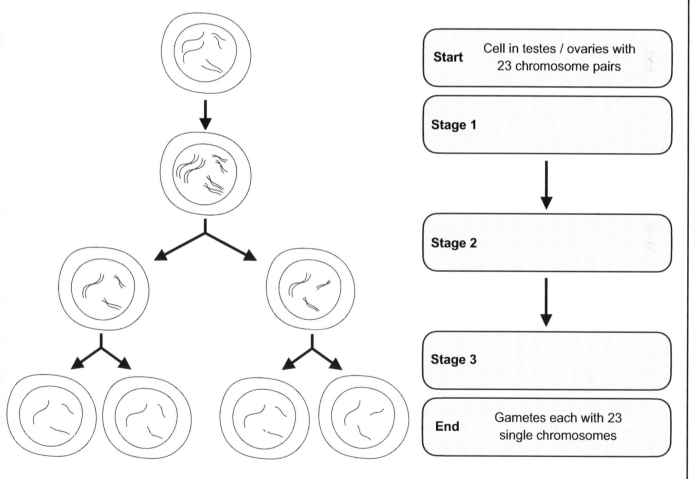

Start — Cell in testes / ovaries with 23 chromosome pairs

Stage 1

Stage 2

Stage 3

End — Gametes each with 23 single chromosomes

d. Complete the sentences below by selecting the correct word from each pair.

Meiosis produces **two / four** gamete cells.

The number of chromosomes is **doubled / halved** compared to the original cell.

Gametes are genetically different as they have different **alleles / genes**.

2. The diagram shows fertilisation taking place (note that only three chromosome pairs are shown).

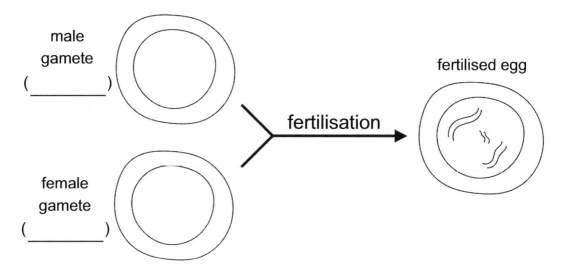

a. Complete the diagram to show the names of the male and female gametes in humans.

b. Complete the male and female gametes to show the chromosomes before fertilisation.

c. Why is it important that meiosis halves the number of chromosomes when producing gametes?

You should refer to fertilisation in your answer.

d. Complete the sentence below.

In meiosis the chromosome number is _____ but in fertilisation it is _____

3. After fertilisation, the fertilised egg undergoes cell division, forming a ball of identical cells.

a. What do scientists call the ball of identical cells?

foetus   embryo   zygote

b. Which type of cell division is taking place?

Write this in the diagram.

Use the diagram to explain your answer.

c. After some time, the cells begin to differentiate.

Describe what is meant by "differentiate".

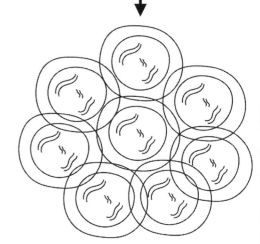

Cell division by

_____

DNA and the Genome

1. The diagram shows a cell. This is not a human cell.

a. Label the diagram to show the nucleus and the chromosomes.

b. How can we tell from the diagram that this cell is not a gamete?

c. Complete the sentences below by using the correct words from the list.

smaller   **helix**   **polymer**   **DNA**   **two**   **inherited**   **genetic**

Chromosomes contain the molecule _____ . Because it

controls our _____ features, DNA is called the _____

material. DNA consists of _____ strands wrapped around each

other. Scientists call this the double _____ . Each strand is made

by joining _____ molecules. Because of this, we say that the

DNA molecule is a _____ .

DNA

d. A gene is a small section on a chromosome.
The diagram shows the gene encoding a protein molecule.
Describe how the instructions in the gene determine the structure of the protein.

Gene

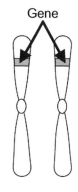

Protein encoded
by gene

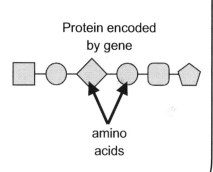

amino
acids

2. Scientists have worked out the genome of humans.

a. Complete the sentence below to explain what is meant by the word "genome".

> The genome is the entire _____ of an organism.

b. Draw lines to link the statements at the top with the correct statements at the bottom.

| Studying the genome allows us to identify the genes which increase the risk of conditions such as ... | Studying the genome helps us to learn about human migration patterns. This is useful for ... | Studying the genome helps us to develop better treatments for inherited conditions such as ... |

| ... determining our ancestry | Cystic Fibrosis | cancer or Alzheimer's disease |

Alleles

1. The diagram shows a pair of human chromosomes.

a. Use the diagram to fill in the gaps below.

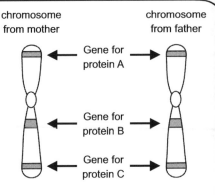

chromosome from mother   chromosome from father

Gene for protein A

Gene for proteln B

Gene for protein C

> We have _____ copies of each chromosome.
>
> We inherit one copy from each of our _____ .
>
> Because of this we have two copies of every _____ .

b. Draw lines to connect the words on the left with the correct definitions on the right.

Alleles ●   ● This person has two copies of the same allele

Genotype ●   ● This allele only determines the phenotype if two copies are present

Homozygous ●   ● This person has two different alleles

Phenotype ●   ● This allele determines the phenotype even if only one copy is present

Heterozygous ●   ● This tells us the alleles that a person has for a given gene

Dominant allele ●   ● These are different versions of a gene

Recessive allele ●   ● This tells us the characteristics caused by a person's alleles

c. Lactose is a sugar found in milk.

In human adults, the ability to digest lactose (D) is dominant to the inability to digest lactose (d).

For the genotypes below, state the person's phenotype and whether they are homozygous or heterozygous.

> **genotype = dd**
>
> Phenotype =
>
> Homozygous / Heterozygous

> **genotype = DD**
>
> Phenotype =
>
> Homozygous / Heterozygous

> **genotype = Dd**
>
> Phenotype =
>
> Homozygous / Heterozygous

d. In mice, black hair (B) is dominant to brown hair (b).

Complete the boxes below to show the missing phenotypes and genotype.

Show whether the mice are homozygous or heterozygous.

> **genotype = Bb**
>
> Phenotype =
>
> Homozygous / Heterozygous

> **genotype =**
>
> Phenotype = brown hair
>
> Homozygous / Heterozygous

> **genotype = BB**
>
> Phenotype =
>
> Homozygous / Heterozygous

e. Give an example of a feature in humans which is controlled by several genes acting together.

Cystic Fibrosis

Exam tip: Remember that unlike cystic fibrosis, most phenotypes are caused by multiple genes acting together. This can explain why not every cross produces simple ratios in the offspring.

1. Cystic fibrosis is a condition caused by a single gene.

a. Which part of the cell is affected by cystic fibrosis?

b. The gene which causes cystic fibrosis has two alleles.

The allele for unaffected (C) is dominant. The allele for cystic fibrosis (c) is recessive.

Connect the genotype with the correct phenotype and show whether the person is homozygous or heterozygous.

CC	This person is a carrier for cystic fibrosis	Homozygous
Cc	This person has cystic fibrosis	Heterozygous
cc	This person is not affected by cystic fibrosis	

2. The Punnett square shows what happens when a carrier for cystic fibrosis has children with a non-affected person.

a. Complete the Punnett square to show the expected genotypes and phenotypes of the offspring.

b. Complete the box to show the expected ratio of offspring which are carriers and which are unaffected.

Carriers : Unaffected

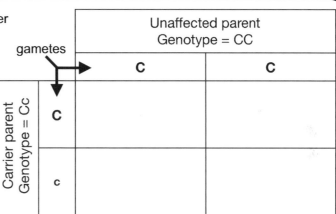

3. The Punnett square shows what happens when two carriers of cystic fibrosis have children.

a. Complete the Punnett square to show the expected genotypes and phenotypes of the offspring.

b. Complete the box to show the expected ratio of offspring.

Unaffected : Carriers : Cystic fibrosis

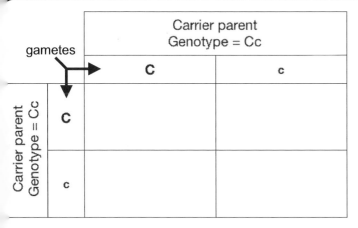

c. Explain why the actual number of offspring with each genotype may not match the ratios predicted above.

Polydactyly

1. Polydactyly is another condition caused by a single gene.

a. How is a person with polydactyly affected?

b. Select the correct words to explain why a person cannot be a carrier of polydactyly.

> Because the polydactyly allele is **recessive / dominant** you only need
>
> **one copy / two copies / three copies** of the allele to have polydactyly.

c. The Punnett square shows a person with polydactyly and a person who is not affected by polydactyly.

Complete the diagram to show the expected genotypes and phenotypes of the offspring.

d. Complete the box to show the ratio of the phenotypes.

> Polydactyly : Unaffected

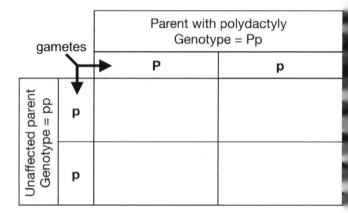

e. Explain why the actual ratio of offspring may not match the ratio predicted by the Punnett square.

---

2. Embryo screening can be used when there is a risk of passing on an inherited disorder.

Complete the sentences below by using the correct words from the list.

economic   desirable   change   destroyed   unethical

healthy   allele   implanted   benefits

In embryo screening, we test embryos for the presence of the defective _____ . Embryos

without the defective allele are _____ into the woman and develop into _____

offspring. Some people feel that the _____ do not justify the cost. This is an _____

issue. In embryo screening, some healthy embryos are _____ . Some people feel that this is

_____ . In the future, gene therapy could allow doctors to _____ alleles to prevent

inherited disorders. However, some people worry that embryo screening and gene therapy could allow

us to select offspring for _____ features. This is a social issue.

Family Trees

1. The allele which leads to cystic fibrosis is recessive.

a. The boxes show three different genotypes involving the cystic fibrosis gene.

In each case, circle the correct phenotype of a person with the genotype shown.

| CC | unaffected
carrier
cystic fibrosis | CC | unaffected
carrier
cystic fibrosis | Cc | unaffected
carrier
cystic fibrosis |

The diagram below shows a family tree involving the cystic fibrosis allele.

☐ male without cystic fibrosis   ○ female without cystic fibrosis   ■ male with cystic fibrosis   ● female with cystic fibrosis

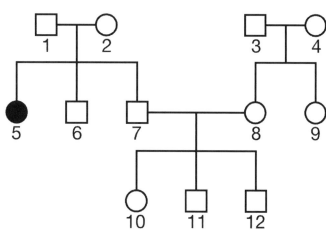

b. State the genotype of person 5.

Explain your answer.

c. How does the family tree prove that cystic fibrosis is caused by a recessive allele?

d. If person 1 and 2 had another child, what is the probability that it would have cystic fibrosis?

e. Can we be certain that persons 7 and 8 are not carriers of the cystic fibrosis allele?

2. The diagram below shows a family tree involving the polydactyly allele.

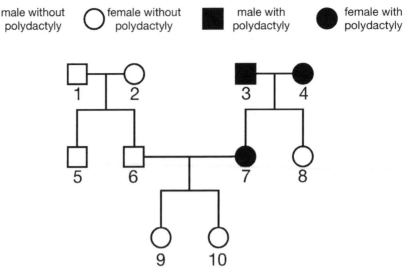

a. Which of the following is the genotype of person 7?

Explain your answer.

(pp)   (pP)   (PP)

b. If person 6 and 7 had one more child, what is the probability that it would have polydactyly?

---

3. Hair length in cats is determined by a gene.

This has an allele for long hair and an allele for short hair.

The diagram shows a family tree for hair length.

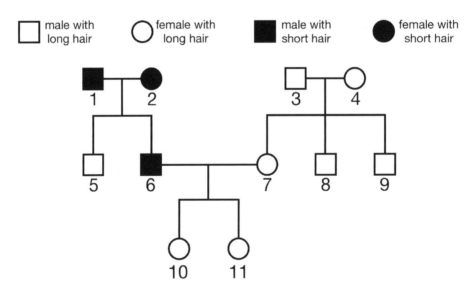

Does the diagram show that the long hair allele is dominant or recessive?

Explain your answer.

Inheritance of Sex

1. A person's sex is determined by the chromosomes they inherit from their parents.

a. Complete the sentences below by circling the correct words.

In humans,
> 21
> 22
> 23

of our chromosome pairs determine our inherited features eg eye colour.

The remaining chromosome pair determines our sex. In males this is
> XX
> XY
> YY

and in females it is
> XX
> XY
> YY

.

b. The Punnett square below shows the sex chromosomes for a couple.

Complete the Punnett square as follow:

- Write the sex chromosomes present in the gametes for the male and the female parents
- Complete the sex chromosome genotypes for the offspring
- Determine whether each offspring is male or female

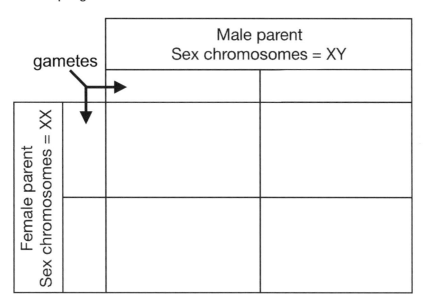

gametes

Male parent
Sex chromosomes = XY

Female parent
Sex chromosomes = XX

c. State the ratio and percentages of males to females predicted by the above Punnett square.

Ratio

> Male : Female

Percentages

> Male : Female

d. Why can the ratio above not be used to predict the number of male or female children in a family?

Chapter 3 : Variation and Evolution

- Describe how variation in the individuals in a population can be due to genetic factors, environmental factors or a combination of both.

- Describe how a mutation can produce a completely new phenotype.

- Describe how evolution by natural selection can lead to a phenotype change in a species.

- Describe how selective breeding can be used to produce plants and animals with desirable genetic features.

- Describe how genetic engineering can be used to produce genetically modified organisms.

- Explain why some people have concerns over genetically modified crops.

- Describe how fossils provide evidence for evolution by natural selection.

- Describe the reasons why a species may become extinct.

- Describe how antibiotic resistant bacteria provide evidence for evolution by natural selection.

- State the seven stages in the classification system developed by Linnaeus.

- Describe the classification system proposed by Carl Woese.

- Describe how an evolutionary tree shows us the evolutionary relationships between different organisms.

Variation

1. We can see a great deal of variation in organisms even between members of the same species.

a. Complete the sentences below by using the correct words from the list.

genetic   eye   diet   language   differences   alleles   height   environment

Variation is all the _____ in the characteristics of individuals in a population. There are

three main causes of variation. Variation can be caused by the _____ that an individual

inherits from their parents. We call this _____ variation and good examples are hair

colour and _____ colour. Some variation is caused by the _____ for

example _____ in humans is affected by the environment in which a child grows up.

Some variation is caused by a mixture of genetic and environmental factors for example a person's

_____ . Some people have alleles which make them likely to grow tall. However, their

final height is also influenced by their _____ which must contain enough calcium.

b. The boxes below describe the variation that we can find in humans.

Suggest whether each is caused by genetics, the environment or a combination.

Explain your answer.

Inherited conditions eg cystic fibrosis	⇨	
Muscle strength	⇨	
Tatoos	⇨	
Infectious diseases eg chicken pox	⇨	
Sun tan	⇨	
Shape of nose	⇨	

2. As we saw in question 1, a lot of variation is caused by our genetics.

All genetic variation is due to mutations.

a. Which of the following is the best definition of a mutation?

> Mutations are predictable changes to DNA taking place all the time

> Mutations are random changes to DNA taking place all the time

> Mutations are random changes to DNA taking place very rarely

b. The three statements below describe mutations.

Draw lines to show whether the statements apply to few, some or many mutations.

Remember that the phenotype is the characteristics caused by an organism's alleles.

> Mutations which have no effect at all on an organism's phenotype

> This only applies to a very small number of mutations

> Mutations which influence phenotype eg tallness alleles lead to tallness if a person's diet is suitable

> This applies to most mutations

> Mutations which directly cause an organism's phenotype eg eye colour in humans

> This applies to some mutations

3. Sometimes a mutation can produce a completely new phenotype.

Read the paragraph and answer the questions below.

> In the 1950s a virus spread from Europe into the UK. This virus was highly infectious and fatal to rabbits. Up to 99% of wild rabbits in the UK died. However, a mutation occurred which made rabbits resistant to the virus. These rabbits survived and reproduced. Over time, the mutation became common in rabbits in the UK.

a. The mutation described leads to a new phenotype in rabbits.

Describe the new phenotype.

b. Explain why the mutation rapidly became common in the UK rabbit population.

Evolution by Natural Selection

1. Scientists think that all living organisms on Earth evolved from a common ancestor.

a. The boxes below describe possible facts about how life started on Earth.

Tick the two boxes that scientists think describe how life started.

Life started on Earth around 30 million years ago	Life started on Earth around 300 million years ago	Life started on Earth around 3 billion years ago
The first living things were complex eg fish	The first living things were simple eg single celled organisms	The first living things were plants on land

b. Variation within a species allows the species to adapt to changes in the environment.

The diagram shows two rabbits. The rabbit on the right has thicker fur than the rabbit on the left.

The boxes below describe how variation allows the rabbits to adapt to cold conditions.

Complete the boxes using the descriptions below.

Every rabbit has a slightly different combination of alleles to other rabbits ⇨

⬇

In cold conditions the rabbits with alleles for thinner fur are less likely to survive ⬅

⬇

The rabbit's offspring could inherit the alleles for thicker fur ⇨

⬇

Over time, the alleles for thicker fur become more common than the alleles for thinner fur ⬅

This means that after many generations the rabbits will have thicker fur than before	**These offspring are also more likely to survive and reproduce than rabbits with thinner fur**	**Rabbits with alleles for thicker fur are more likely to survive the cold conditions and reproduce**	**For example one rabbit may have alleles for thicker fur than other rabbits**

2. We have seen how different alleles allow individuals to survive when the environment changes.

Over time, these alleles become more common in a species.

a. What name do scientists give to this process?

Natural selection   Artificial selection   Selective breeding

As well as fur length, rabbits can also show variation in fur colour.

A rabbit's alleles can make their fur dark or white.

b. Foxes are a natural predator for rabbits.

Complete the boxes to show what will happen to the rabbit population if the climate changes and snow is permanently on the ground.

Allele for   **dark / white**   fur becomes more common

Allele for   **dark / white**   fur becomes less common

Explain your answer.

c. We can see that in cold and snowy conditions, the rabbit population has evolved.

Complete the definition of evolution below by filling in the missing word.

Evolution is the _____ in the inherited characteristics of a population

over time through a process of natural selection.

3. Sometimes evolution by natural selection can cause dramatic changes in phenotype.

Describe how this can cause a population to split into two separate species.

Selective Breeding

1. Selective breeding (artificial selection) is used to breed plants and animals with desirable genetic features.

a. For the examples, describe the desirable feature being selected.

Food crops	Cattle such as cows

Domestic dogs to be used as pets	Garden plants

b. Imagine that a farmer wanted to use selective breeding to produce sheep with very soft wool.

The stages are shown below. Write them in the correct order in the boxes on the right.

The farmer would then select the offspring with the softest wool	1
The farmer would breed these sheep together	2
The farmer would then allow these offspring to breed	3
After many generations of selective breeding all the sheep would have soft wool	4
The farmer would take a mixed group of sheep	5
The farmer would select the male and female sheep with the softest wool	6

c. In selective breeding, closely related organisms are bred together.

Explain why this can be a problem.

Genetic Engineering

1. Genetic engineering is used extensively to modify plants and microorganisms such as bacteria.

a. The diagram shows a gene and the protein it encodes.

Describe how the gene controls the structure of the protein.

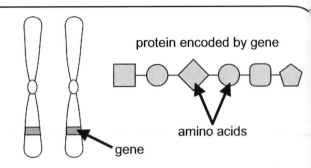

b. Complete the sentences below by using the correct words from the list.

insulin   bacteria   diabetes   glucose   transfer   cut   genome   human

To carry out genetic engineering, we first _____ out the gene from one organism for

example a human and then _____ the gene to cells of a different organism for example

a bacterium. We have modified the _____ of the bacterium so that it now includes a

_____ gene. A good example of genetic engineering is _____ . This is

used to control the level of the sugar _____ in a person's blood. People with type 1

_____ cannot make their own insulin. The human insulin gene has been cut out and

transferred to _____ . These can now make the human insulin used by type 1 diabetics.

2. Genetic engineering of plants produces genetically modified (GM) crops.

a. Describe two advantages of GM crops over unmodified crops.

b. Some GM crops are not killed by herbicides (weed killers).
Describe the benefit of this to farmers.

c. Describe why some people wonder whether GM crops are safe.

3. Genetic engineering of humans could treat inherited disorders. This is called gene therapy.
Describe why some people question the long term safety of gene therapy.

4. The diagram shows the stages that take place during genetic engineering.

a. State three types of organism where the gene of interest could be found.

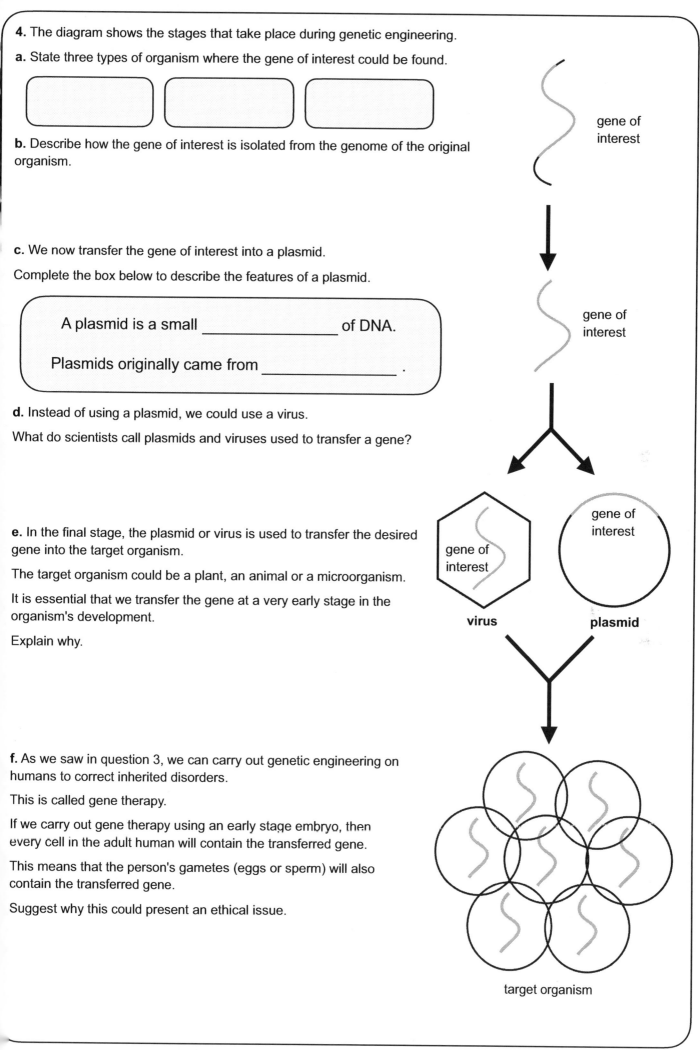

gene of interest

b. Describe how the gene of interest is isolated from the genome of the original organism.

c. We now transfer the gene of interest into a plasmid.

Complete the box below to describe the features of a plasmid.

A plasmid is a small _____ of DNA.

Plasmids originally came from _____ .

gene of interest

d. Instead of using a plasmid, we could use a virus.

What do scientists call plasmids and viruses used to transfer a gene?

e. In the final stage, the plasmid or virus is used to transfer the desired gene into the target organism.

The target organism could be a plant, an animal or a microorganism.

It is essential that we transfer the gene at a very early stage in the organism's development.

Explain why.

gene of interest

gene of interest

virus   **plasmid**

f. As we saw in question 3, we can carry out genetic engineering on humans to correct inherited disorders.

This is called gene therapy.

If we carry out gene therapy using an early stage embryo, then every cell in the adult human will contain the transferred gene.

This means that the person's gametes (eggs or sperm) will also contain the transferred gene.

Suggest why this could present an ethical issue.

target organism

Evidence for Evolution: Fossils

1. Fossils give us a lot of information about how organisms have evolved.

a. Complete the sentence below to give the definition of a fossil.

Fossils are the [   ] of organisms from millions

of years ago which are found in [   ]

b. The boxes below show the three ways that fossils can form.

Link the boxes on the left with the correct descriptions on the right.

Fossils can form if parts of an organism do not decay	This includes animal footprints or burrows and spaces in the soil where plant roots were
Fossils can form while an organism decays	Decay cannot take place in cold conditions or where there is not enough oxygen or water present
Fossils can be the traces of organisms	In this case, minerals slowly replace parts of the organism during the decay process

2. Scientists cannot be certain how life on Earth began.

This is because there are very few fossils of the earliest forms of life on Earth.

a. Explain why the earliest life forms were unlikely to form fossils.

b. Describe how a large amount of the fossils that were formed will have been destroyed.

3. Most species that were on Earth are now extinct.

That means that there are no members of that species alive.

Give an example of the following three ways that extinction can happen.

Catastrophe	Environmental change	Competition

Evidence for Evolution: Resistant Bacteria

1. Many bacteria are pathogens for example those that cause salmonella food poisoning.

Complete the sentences below by circling the correct words.

Because antibiotics [disable / inhibit / kill] bacteria they are used to prevent bacterial diseases. Antibiotics are also used

on farms to prevent bacterial diseases in [plants / animals / vegetables] . Under ideal conditions, bacteria reproduce every twenty

[seconds / minutes / hours] . Because they reproduce at a fast rate, bacteria can evolve rapidly. Recently bacteria have evolved

which are no longer killed by antibiotics. These are called [antibiotic resistant / antibiotic immune / antibiotic protected] bacteria eg MRSA.

2. The diagram below shows how an antibiotic resistant bacterium can develop and spread.

a. Use the boxes below to describe the stages shown.

antibiotic

| The bacterium becomes resistant to antibiotics | There is no competition from non-resistant bacteria | The antibiotic resistant bacterium reproduces |

| A random mutation occurs | All the non-resistant bacteria die | An antibiotic is applied to the bacteria |

b. Explain why antibiotic resistant bacteria can spread rapidly through a population.

c. We need to reduce the chances that bacteria become resistant to antibiotics. This is because developing new antibiotics costs a lot of money and takes many years.

One way is by reducing the use of antibiotics on farms.

The boxes show two other ways of reducing the development of antibiotic resistant bacteria.

In each case, explain how these reduce the chances of antibiotic resistance developing.

Only prescribe antibiotics where appropriate	Always complete a course of antibiotics

Classification

Exam tip: In the exam, you could be asked about the classification of an organism. All the information that you need about that organism will be given in the question.

1. Classification involves grouping organisms based on features they have in common.

One of the first scientists to do this was Carl Linnaeus.

a. Linnaeus divided all organisms into two kingdoms. Complete the boxes to show the kingdoms he used.

 Two kingdoms used by Linnaeus

b. At the time of Linnaeus, many organisms had not been discovered.

Give the name of a type of organism which we now know does not fit into Linnaeus's two kingdom system.

c. There are seven stages to Linnaeus's classification system. These are shown below.

Complete the boxes to show a mnemonic that you could use to memorise this system.

(kingdom) (phylum) (class) (order) (family) (genus) (species)

( ) ( ) ( ) ( ) ( ) ( ) ( )

d. The classification systems of three organisms are shown below.

In each case, complete the boxes to show the missing words.

Garlic	**Red kangaroo**	**Wolf**
Kingdom = _____	Kingdom = _____	Kingdom = _____
Phylum = Magnoliophyta	_____ = Chordata	Phylum = Chordata
Class = Liliopsida	Class = Mammalia	_____ = Mammalia
_____ = Liliales	Order = Diprotodonia	Order = Carnivora
Family = Liliaceae	_____ = Macropodidae	Family = Canidae
Genus = Allium	Genus = Macropus	_____ = Canis
Species = sativum	Species = rufus	Species = lupus

e. Each organism has a binomial name.

How do we work out the binomial name for an organism?

f. State the binomial names for the three organisms shown above.

Garlic	**Red kangaroo**	**Wolf**

2. Linnaeus's classification system was based on similar features that scientists could see.

Now scientists can use microscopes to look for similarities in internal structures such as organs.

They can also look at similarities in molecules for example in DNA or proteins.

The structure of a protein is shown below for three different organisms.

Organism A	Organism B	Organism C

a. Explain how the protein structures show that organisms A and B are closely related.

b. Explain how they show that organism C is not closely related to organisms A or B.

c. The scientist Carl Woese used information about molecules to develop the three domain system.

Complete the boxes to describe the three domains.

Archae	True bacteria	Eukaryota
Primitive bacteria often found in _____ conditions eg hot springs	These are found in places such as the human digestive _____	This domain includes animals, plants, fungi and protists such as_____

3. An evolutionary tree shows us how related different organisms are to each other.

For living organisms, scientists can use information such as DNA sequences.

a. How do scientists place extinct organisms on an evolutionary tree?

The evolutionary tree below shows five species of primates (including humans).

b. Which primates are most closely related to humans?

Explain your answer.

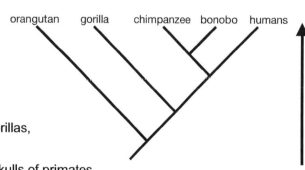

c. On the evolutionary tree show the common ancestor of gorillas, chimpanzees, bonobos and humans.

d. A scientist found a fossilised skull that was similar to the skulls of primates.

Suggest why it might be difficult to place this species on the primate evolutionary tree.

Chapter 4 : Ecology

- Describe how different organisms compete for the same resources.

- Describe what is meant by interdependence and a stable community.

- Describe what is meant by biotic and abiotic factors and give examples.

- Describe what is meant by structural, functional and behavioural adaptations and give examples for plants and animals.

- Describe what is meant by a producer, primary consumer, secondary consumer and tertiary consumer and how they interact in a food chain.

- Describe the importance of producers in a food chain and what is meant by biomass.

- Describe how the number of predator and prey change and interpret a predator-prey cycle.

- Describe how to sample organisms using a quadrat in both random sampling and in sampling along a transect.

- Describe how to use random sampling to estimate the population size of a species.

- Describe how to carry out the required practical on sampling organisms.

- Describe how to calculate the mean, the median and the mode from a given set of numbers.

- Describe the main stages of the carbon cycle and the water cycle.

- Describe what is meant by biodiversity and explain why a rich diversity is important for an ecosystem.

- Describe how biodiversity can be threatened by waste management, including sewage, air pollution and landfills.

- Describe how humans use land and how this can contribute to a reduction in biodiversity.

- Describe how human activity leads to an increase in atmospheric levels of carbon dioxide and methane.

- Describe what we can do to protect biodiversity, including wetlands management, breeding programs for endangered species and recycling.

Competition and Interdependence

1. Ecologists study how the organisms in a habitat depend on each other.

a. Draw lines to connect the words on the left to the correct definitions and examples on the right.

| Habitat | The populations of all the different species living in the same habitat | A tropical rainforest |

| Population | This is the environment in which an organism lives | All of the populations in a tropical rainforest |

| Community | The living organisms in an ecosystem | All the animals, plants, insects and bacteria in a rainforest |

| Ecosystem | The number of organisms of the same species living in the same geographical area | The animals, plants, water and minerals in a rainforest |

| Biotic | The non-living parts of an ecosystem | All of the Eastern Gorillas living in Rwanda |

| Abiotic | The living and non-living parts of an environment and how they interact | All the water and minerals in a rainforest |

b. Plants and animals compete for limited resources in an ecosystem.

Next to each resource below, write "A" if it is competed for by animals and "P" if it is competed for by plants.

Light   **Food**   **Mates**   **Territory**   **Space**   **Water**   **Minerals**

c. The organisms in an ecosystem depend on each other in a large number of different ways.

What do scientists call this?

| Interdependence | Interaction | Intercommunity |

d. Complete the boxes below to show how organisms can depend on each other.

| Animals depending on animals | Animals depending on plants | Plants depending on animals |

e. If all of the bees in a habitat die, this could cause the populations of animals to fall. Explain how.

f. Explain what is meant by a stable community.

Biotic and Abiotic Factors

1. The first biotic factor is the availability of food.

a. In Africa, lions eat other animals including zebra. Zebra eat plants such as grass.

Using these examples, explain why food is a biotic factor.

b. A drought can cause the amount of grass to decrease.

Explain how this would affect both the population of zebra and the population of lions.

2. The Nile Perch is a fish found in Africa. An adult Nile Perch can reach 2 metres in length.

a. In the descriptions below, circle which type of biotic factor is being described and explain your answer.

In the 1950s Nile Perch were released into Africa's Lake Victoria.

The Nile Perch ate native fish causing the populations to collapse.

In Australia it was decided not to release Nile Perch into the wild.

This is because Nile Perch eat the same prey species as the native fish the Barramundi.

Biotic factor = predation / competition

Biotic factor = predation / competition

b. The Bilby is a small burrowing animal found in Australia.

The numbers of Bilby have fallen since rabbits were brought to Australia over 200 years ago.

Rabbits can compete with Bilbies for food and burrows.

Describe what could happen to the Bilby if they are not protected.

c. In 1950 a virus was deliberately released in Australia. This virus kills rabbits.

This caused rabbit numbers to fall.

Describe how this is an example of a biotic factor.

3. As well as biotic factors, abiotic factors also affect both plants and animals. Abiotic factors are shown below.

a. Write "P" if the factor applies to plants, "A" if it applies to animals and "B" if it applies to both plants and animals.

Light intensity

Wind intensity and direction

Carbon dioxide level

Oxygen level

Temperature

Water

Soil pH and minerals

b. As woods grow, smaller shrubs are overshadowed by taller trees.

Describe the effect of this on the smaller shrubs and on animals which eat these shrubs.

c. Temperature change can also affect plants and animals. Complete the box below to describe this.

If the temperature changes, species of plants may _____ entirely from a habitat.

Animals may _____ (move to a different location).

d. Animals and plants cannot survive without water. State a function of water in animals and in plants.

Animals _____

Plants _____

e. Give an example of a mineral needed by plants and explain what it is used for.

f. Explain why plants growing in sand dunes are adapted to deal with water loss.

g. Plants grow slowly if the level of carbon dioxide in the air falls. Explain why.

h. Oxygen levels can strongly affect aquatic organisms such as fish. Tick the box which best explains why.

Aquatic organisms use more oxygen than land-based animals

The amount of oxygen dissolved in water decreases sharply in warm conditions

Too much oxygen is harmful to fish

Adaptations

1. Camels are adapted to the hot conditions of the desert, where water is very scarce.

Camels show a number of structural adaptations. These are shown in the diagram below.

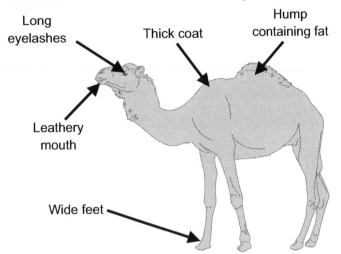

Long eyelashes

Thick coat

Hump containing fat

Leathery mouth

Wide feet

a. Describe what is meant by a structural adaptation.

b. Explain why the camel's fat is in the hump rather than being spread around the body.

c. Complete the boxes to show the purpose of the following structural adaptations.

Thick coat on upper surface of body	Leathery interior of mouth
Long eyelashes	Wide feet

d. As well as structural adaptations, camels also have a number of functional adaptations.

Describe what is meant by a functional adaptation.

e. Describe two functional adaptations in camels.

2. Other desert animals show behavioural adaptations. A good example is the kangaroo rat.

a. What is meant by behavioural adaptations?

b. The kangaroo rat is nocturnal (active only at night). It spends the daytime in a burrow.

Explain the purpose of these behavioural adaptations.

3. The Arctic Fox is adapted to live in cold, snowy conditions.

The diagram shows the adaptations of the Arctic Fox.

a. In winter, the Arctic Fox has white fur.

Explain the benefit of this.

Very small
ears

Thick white
fur

Fur on soles
of feet

b. The other adaptations of the Artic Fox reduce the amount of heat energy lost to the cold environment.

Draw a line to link each adaptation with the correct description below.

| Thick fur on body | Fur on soles of feet | Very small ears |

| This reduces heat loss to the ice and snow | This reduces the surface area of the fox, reducing heat loss to the air | This insulates the fox's body and reduces loss of heat to the air |

spines

water stored
in stem

4. Cacti are plants which are adapted to living in the hot and dry conditions of the desert.

a. Describe the main issue faced by plants living in the desert.

b. Complete the boxes below to show the purpose of the following adaptations found in cacti.

| Water stored in stem | Extensive and shallow roots | Very small leaves or spines |

5. Bacteria can be found living in vents on the sea bed.

These bacteria are adapted to extreme conditions.

a. What do scientists call organisms which are adapted to live in extreme conditions?

| Extreme-loving | Extremophiles | Extremophobes |

b. Describe three extreme conditions that can be faced by these organisms.

Food Chains and Predator-Prey Cycles

1. Food chains tell us how different organisms feed on each other in an ecosystem.

Two food chains are shown below. We would find these organisms in the UK.

Seaside food chain

Algae → Common periwinkle → Brown crab → Octopus

Countryside food chain

Grass → Rabbit → Stoat → Fox

a. Complete the sentences below by using the correct words from the list.

photosynthesis   biomass   producer   sunlight   algae   glucose

Every food chain starts with a _____ . This can be a green plant such as grass or it could

be an _____ such as seaweed. All producers carry out _____ to produce

the complex molecule _____ . To do this, they use the energy from _____ .

Scientists call molecules such as glucose _____ . This is passed along the food chain.

b. Link the words to the correct descriptions.

Then give examples from the food chains above.

This is an animal which eats a primary consumer.	Producer	
This is an animal which eats a secondary consumer.	Primary consumer	
This is an animal which eats a producer.	Secondary consumer	
This carries out photosynthesis, using energy from sunlight to make glucose.	Tertiary consumer	

c. A predator is an animal which kills and eats another animal (which we call the prey).

Name the animals which are shown in the above food chains as ...

Prey animals only	Both prey and predators	Predator animals only

2. A predator-prey cycle shows us how the levels of predator and prey animals change over time.

The diagram shows the predator-prey cycle for stoat (predator) and rabbit (prey).

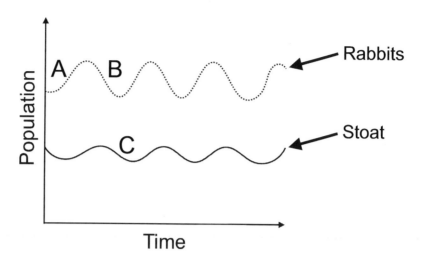

a. Point A on the graph shows a warm summer.

Explain how this affects the population of rabbits.

b. How does the warm summer affect the population of stoat?

c. What is happening to the population of rabbits at point B? Explain your answer.

d. Explain why the population of stoat fell at point C.

e. Describe how the fall in the stoat population will affect the rabbit population. Explain your answer.

f. We find predator-prey cycles just like this one when the community is stable.

Complete the box below to show what this means.

In a stable community the _____ and abiotic factors are in _____ .

g. Stoat also eat weasels. One year, the weasel population increased sharply. Weasels do not eat grass.

Suggest how this could affect the population of rabbits.

Sampling Organisms

1. We can sample organisms by random sampling and sampling along a transect.

Both methods use a quadrat.

a. Describe what is meant by a quadrat and explain how we use it.

b. Circle the organisms that could be sampled using a quadrat and explain your answer below.

birds   dandelions   snails   rabbits   daisies   limpets

c. Random sampling is used to compare the numbers of organisms in two different areas.

For example, we could compare the numbers of dandelions in a marshy field and a well-drained field.

To do this, we throw the quadrat randomly a number of times.

Describe one way to throw the quadrat randomly.

d. Explain why it is important that we throw the quadrat randomly.

e. Why do we throw the quadrat a large number of times in each location?

2. We can use a quadrat to estimate the total population of an organism in a location.

To do that, we use the equation below.

$$\text{Total population size} = \frac{\text{Total area}}{\text{Area sampled}} \times \text{Number of organisms of that species counted in sample}$$

A scientist wanted to estimate the number of dandelions in a field.

They used a quadrat with an area of 0.25 m². They threw the quadrat ten times and counted 380 dandelions.

The total area of the habitat was 1000 m². Calculate the total population of dandelions.

3. Sampling along a transect is used to see if the numbers of a species change moving across a location.

a. For each of the following questions state whether we would use random sampling or sampling along a transect.

How many snails are in a garden?	How does the number of daisies change as we get further away from a tree?	What is the population of limpets on a rocky shore?	How does the species of plants change as we cross a sand dune?

b. The following boxes show the stages in carrying out sampling along a transect.

Place the stages in the correct order.

Repeat until you reach the end of the tape measure	Identify the species in the quadrat using a guide	Select the habitat that you are going to sample
Count the number of each species again	Move the tape measure along the habitat and repeat	Count the numbers of the different species present
Place a quadrat at the start of the tape measure	Place a tape measure across the habitat	Move the quadrat 1m along the tape measure

The diagram below shows sampling along a transect on a sand dune.

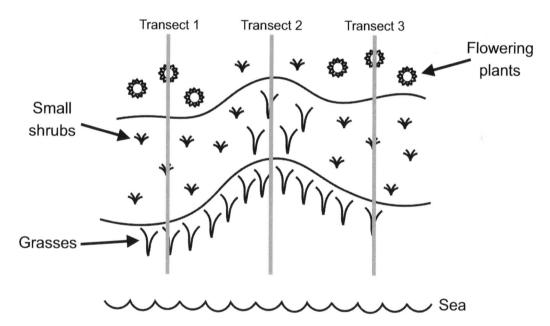

c. Describe how the results of transect 2 are different to transects 1 and 3.

d. Using the results above, explain why it is important that we perform a transect a number of times.

Required Practical: Sampling

1. First we are going to estimate the population of an organism in a habitat. The method is shown below.

- Place two tape measures at right angles along the edges of the habitat.
- Write the numbers 1-20 on pieces of paper and place in a bag.
- One student selects a number and moves to that position on the first tape measure.
- Another student selects a number and moves to that position on the second tape measure.
- A third student places a quadrat at the point where the numbers meet.
- The student counts the number of each species in the quadrat.
- The process is repeated for a total of ten times.

a. Which method of sampling is being used?   **Random Sampling**   **Sampling along a transect**

b. Explain the importance of using random numbers in this experiment.

c. The students counted snails. They used a 0.25m² quadrat which they threw ten times. They found 730 snails. The total area of the habitat was 550m². Estimate the total number of snails.

d. Explain why this figure is only an estimate.

2. In the second part, we estimate how the number of a species changes across a habitat.

For example how does the number of snails change as we move out of a wood and into a field?

Our hypothesis is that the number of snails decreases as the light intensity increases.

a. Describe how we would carry this out using a tape measure, a quadrat and a light meter.

b. Complete the sentence below by selecting the correct words.

Light intensity is (a biotic   /   an abiotic) factor

c. Suggest how the population of snails could depend on other biotic and abiotic factors.

Mean, Median and Mode

1. To calculate the mean, we add all of our numbers together and then divide by the number of numbers.

Remember that any anomalous results should not be included.

Exam tip: Remember to press equals on your calculator after you have added the numbers together

A student measured the length in mm of five seedlings. These are shown below.

| 62 | 86 | 73 | 101 | 113 |

Exam tip: Remember that the mean has to lie between the smallest and largest numbers

a. Do you think that any of the results are anomalous? Explain your answer.

b. Calculate the mean value.

Mean =

c. A scientist counted the number of woodlice under five different rocks. The results are shown below. Calculate the mean value.

| 12 | 16 | 10 | 18 | 42 |

Mean =

2. The median is the middle number of a set of values.

a. A student counted the number of seeds in five tomatoes. Determine the median value.

| 43 | 26 | 14 | 35 | 19 |

Median =

b. The student measured the length in mm of four of the seeds. Calculate the median value.

| 7 | 8 | 10 | 12 |

Median =

3. The mode is the most frequent number.

a. Determine the mode of the following numbers.

| 8 | 2 | 6 | 8 | 5 | 6 | 1 | 6 |

Mode =

b. Explain why there is no mode for the following values.

| 12 | 9 | 16 | 19 | 14 | 20 | 7 |

The Carbon Cycle

1. The carbon cycle is based around two key processes: photosynthesis and aerobic respiration.

a. Write "P" if the description below applies to photosynthesis and "R" if the description applies to aerobic respiration.

> This returns carbon dioxide back to the atmosphere

> This is only carried out by plants

> This produces the carbon-containing molecule glucose

> Glucose is broken down releasing energy and carbon dioxide

> This is carried out by animals and plants all the time

> Light energy is used to react carbon dioxide and water

> This is the only way that carbon enters the carbon cycle

b. The diagram below shows the stages of the carbon cycle.

Fill in the boxes using the labels provided.

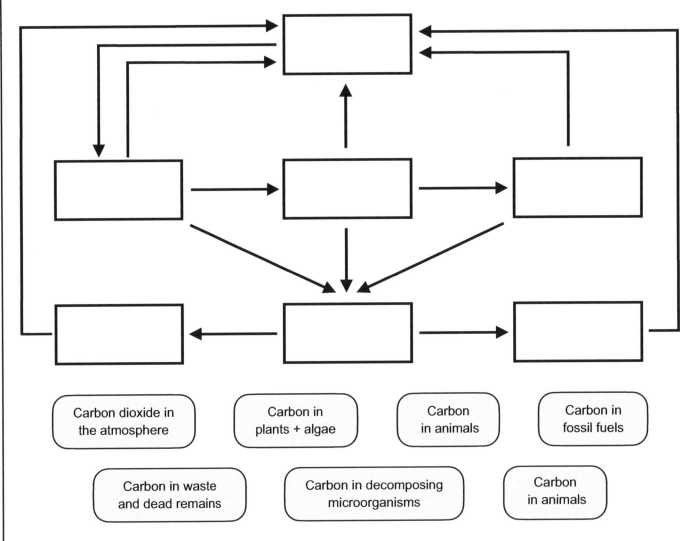

> Carbon dioxide in the atmosphere

> Carbon in plants + algae

> Carbon in animals

> Carbon in fossil fuels

> Carbon in waste and dead remains

> Carbon in decomposing microorganisms

> Carbon in animals

c. Label the arrows to show the processes taking place.

Use the labels below.

- Photosynthesis
- Respiration
- Feeding
- Combustion
- Formation of fossil fuels

Exam tip: It is important to learn the carbon cycle. Remember that a large part of the carbon cycle involves either photosynthesis or aerobic respiration.

2. During the carbon cycle, carbon atoms pass from one living organism to another.

a. Complete the box to describe how carbon passes into the cycle.

Carbon enters the carbon cycle from the _____ when plants carry out _____

b. Describe how carbon atoms pass into animals.

c. State three carbon-containing molecules that we find in both plants and animals.

3. Decomposers play a critical role in the carbon cycle.

a. Complete the sentences below by using the correct words from the list.

respire   oxygen   combusted   fungi   mineral   faeces   fossil   die   atmosphere

All animals release waste products including urine and _____ . Eventually, all animals and

plants _____ . Waste products and dead remains are then broken down by decomposing

microorganisms such as _____ and bacteria. When these decomposers _____

they release carbon dioxide back into the _____ . Decomposers are also important because

they release _____ ions back into the soil. Under certain conditions, for example when there

is not enough _____ , decomposers cannot function. Now the carbon in dead remains is

slowly converted to _____ fuels. When these are _____ (burned), the carbon

is returned back to the atmosphere as carbon dioxide.

b. The statements on the left are incorrect.

Write the correct version in the boxes on the right.

Incorrect statements   **Correct statements**

Breathing produces carbon dioxide from glucose

Only animals carry out respiration

The Water Cycle

1. Water moves around different parts of the Earth in the Water Cycle.

The diagrams below show the stages of the water cycle.

Complete the diagrams using the words below.

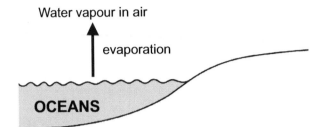

Almost all of the water on Earth is in the oceans.

This is _____ water. Energy from the Sun

makes the water _____ from the surface.

The water vapour in the air cools down. This now

_____ to form clouds. The water now

falls to the ground as _____ eg rain.

Rain water is _____ water (not salty).

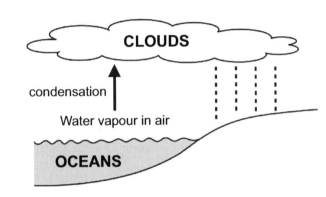

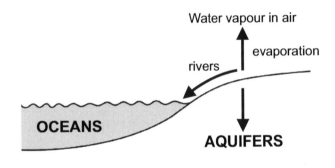

Once the water hits the ground, some of the water

evaporates back to _____ in the air and

some drains through rocks into _____.

A lot of water forms streams and _____.

aquifers   rivers   water vapour   precipitation   condenses   salt   fresh   evaporate

---

2. Water also passes through plants and animals.

a. Circle the correct words to show how water passes through plants.

Water enters the roots and moves up the (xylem / phloem) to the leaves. Water vapour passes

out of the (waxy cuticle / stomata.) This process is called (perspiration / transpiration.)

b. Describe how water passes into and out of animals.

Water passes into animals by

Water passes out of animals by

Biodiversity

Exam tip: Human activity has a very negative impact on biodiversity. I would not be surprised to see a question on biodiversity in the exam.

1. It is really important that humans work hard to preserve the biodiversity on the Earth.

a. Circle the box below to show the best definition of biodiversity.

The variety of different habitats found on the Earth	The variety of all the different species of organisms on Earth	The variety of all the different plants and animals on Earth

b. Complete the sentences below by using the correct words from the list.

Arctic   **falls**   **ecosystem**   **decomposers**   **stable**   **carbon**   **food**   **bacteria**

Biodiversity refers to all the different species of plants, animals, _____ and fungi that we

find on planet Earth. We can also look at the biodiversity found within a single _____ for

example the Amazon rainforest or the _____ circle. Many different species depend on

each other for example as a source of _____ or for shelter eg trees. Many species help to

maintain the environment for example _____ such as bacteria or fungi. These break

down the remains of dead organisms and are important in the _____ cycle. If there are lots

of different species then an ecosystem is more _____. In this case, if the population of one

of the species _____ sharply, then this is less likely to affect the whole ecosystem.

2. Tropical forests for example in the Amazon and in Indonesia are being destroyed.
This is called deforestation and is often carried out to provide land.
a. Explain why the loss of these forests is extremely damaging to planet Earth.

b. One way to reduce deforestation is to reduce meat consumption eg beef. Explain why.

c. In many countries petrol and diesel are being replaced with biofuels which contribute less to climate change.
Explain how this may lead to increased deforestation.

Waste Management

1. The waste that humans produce has a major negative effect on biodiversity for example in streams and rivers.

a. Complete the box below to describe the waste found in untreated human sewage.

> Untreated human sewage contains both (⬚) and (⬚).
>
> These are rich in carbon and nitrogen, which bacteria can use as a source of nutrients.

b. The boxes below describe how untreated sewage can reduce biodiversity.

Rewrite the statements in the correct order in the boxes on the right.

Dissolved oxygen levels in the water fall sharply	
Bacteria use the molecules in the sewage as a source of nutrients and reproduce	
Bacteria use a large amount of oxygen for aerobic respiration	
Aquatic organisms die due to lack of oxygen in the water	
Untreated sewage is accidentally released into rivers or streams	

c. Give two other examples of substances that can reduce biodiversity in streams and rivers.

2. Waste from human activities can also pollute the air and the land.

This also reduces the levels of biodiversity on planet Earth.

Complete the boxes below to show how pollution of the air and land can reduce biodiversity.

Burning coal in power stations	Dumping waste in landfills

Land Use

1. Humans have an increasing need for available land. The effect of this is to reduce biodiversity.

a. Draw lines to link the land use with the purpose on the right.

Land for buildings	These are used to extract minerals from the ground eg for building materials and metal ores for industry.
Land for quarries	These are used to dump unwanted waste materials that cannot be recycled eg from homes and factories.
Land for farming	This includes houses, shops, factories, businesses and transport links such as airports and train stations.
Land for landfills	This is for agriculture eg growing crops or grazing animals for food and to produce milk.

b. Explain how all of these uses of land reduce biodiversity.

2. Peat bogs are found in many parts of the world and contain a very large amount of trapped carbon.

Peat bogs can form when plant material builds up and decays very slowly.

a. Which of the following conditions would cause a very slow rate of decay? Circle one box.

Warm conditions	Damp conditions	Very low levels of oxygen

b. Peat bogs are being destroyed and the peat taken away.

Complete the boxes below to describe how the peat is being used.

Peat is used to make ( ) for gardens and burned to release ( )

c. Circle the correct words below to explain how the destruction of peat bogs harms the environment.

When peat is used for compost it begins to decay, releasing

oxygen
carbon dioxide
nitrogen

. This is also released when we

react
decay
burn

peat to generate electricity. Both of these contribute to climate change. We should stop using peat

for compost on farms. However, the alternatives are expensive and could

increase
decrease
affect

food prices.

Global Warming

1. The average temperature of the Earth's atmosphere is increasing. Many scientists believe that this is due to human activity causing the release of greenhouse gases such as carbon dioxide and methane.

a. Circle the correct boxes to show how these gases are produced.

Burning coal to generate electricity	Produces carbon dioxide	Produces methane
Cows passing wind	Produces carbon dioxide	Produces methane
Burning petrol to power cars	Produces carbon dioxide	Produces methane
Burning gas to heat homes	Produces carbon dioxide	Produces methane
Bacteria in paddy fields where rice is grown	Produces carbon dioxide	Produces methane

b. Scientific research undergoes a process called "peer review".

Describe what is meant by "peer review" and explain why scientific research is more likely to be correct than newspaper articles or websites covering global warming.

2. Global warming will have major effects on species around the world.

Use the words below to complete the boxes describing the possible effects of global warming.

mosquitoes   UK   countries   birds   extinct   habitats   earlier   insects

Global warming will lead to _____ being destroyed. Some organisms will decrease in number or may become _____ .

Animals such as _____ may extend their range to find cooler conditions. These include _____ which can transmit malaria.

As the Earth's temperature increases, animals such as _____ may migrate at different times or to different _____ .

Plants may flower _____ . Crops may grow in the _____ that do not grow now. Some countries may be too hot to grow crops they need.

Maintaining Biodiversity

1. Biodiversity is all the different species of living organisms that we find on planet Earth or in an ecosystem.

It is important that we try to preserve as much biodiversity as possible. Circle the correct answers to explain why.

A rich biodiversity means that any species is (more / less) dependent

on any other species so the ecosystem is (more / less) stable.

2. There are five ways that we can maintain biodiversity.

a. Some species are extremely rare with only a few hundred individuals remaining including those in zoos.

How can zoos help to prevent rare species from going extinct?

b. In the past, large areas of wetlands in the UK were drained to grow crops.

Now many of these areas are being allowed to flood again. Describe the benefit of preserving wetlands.

c. Farmers can also help to increase biodiversity. Complete the sentences below by filling in the spaces.

Farms do not have a lot of biodiversity as fields usually contain only _____ type of crop.

Leaving field margins or planting _____ helps as many different species can live there.

d. Governments can help to maintain biodiversity by reducing deforestation and carbon dioxide emissions.

Complete the boxes to describe how governments can do this.

Reducing deforestation

Reducing carbon dioxide emissions

e. Individuals can help preserve biodiversity by recycling household waste. Describe how this helps.

Biology Paper 2
Combined Science (Higher)

GCSE Specimen Paper

Time allowed: 75 minutes

Maximum marks: 70

Please note that this is a specimen exam paper written by freesciencelessons. The questions are meant to reflect the style of questions that you might see in your GCSE Biology exam.

Neither the exam paper nor the mark scheme have been endorsed by any exam board. The answers are my best estimates of what would be accepted but I cannot guarantee that this would be the case. I do not offer any guarantee that the level you achieve in this specimen paper is the level that you will achieve in the real exam.

1   Camels live in sandy deserts where the conditions are hot during the daytime and drinking water is hard to find.

Figure 1 shows the structural adaptations that help a camel to survive in the desert.

Figure 1

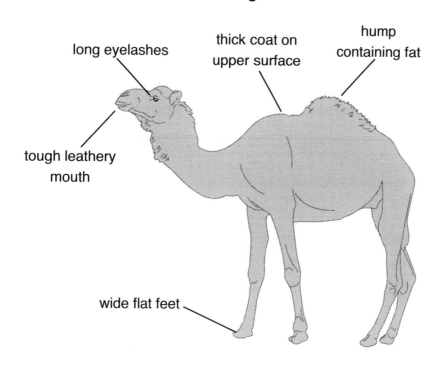

long eyelashes

thick coat on upper surface

hump containing fat

tough leathery mouth

wide flat feet

1 . 1   Describe how the camel's structural adaptations allow it to survive in the desert.

5 marks

_____

_____

_____

_____

_____

_____

_____

_____

_____

1.2   The body temperature of camels can vary widely, ranging from 34°C at night to 40°C during the day.

What name do scientists give to this type of adaptation?

1 mark

Tick **one** box.

Structural adaptation ☐

Behavioural adaptation ☐

Functional adaptation ☐

1.3   Camels can drink rapidly when they find a source of drinking water.

A camel had a mass of 520 kg. It drank a large volume of water and its mass increased to 650 kg.

Calculate the percentage increase in the mass of the camel.

3 marks

Percentage change in mass = _____ %

Total = 9

2   **Figure 2** shows a food chain found in the UK countryside.

Figure 2
(not to scale)

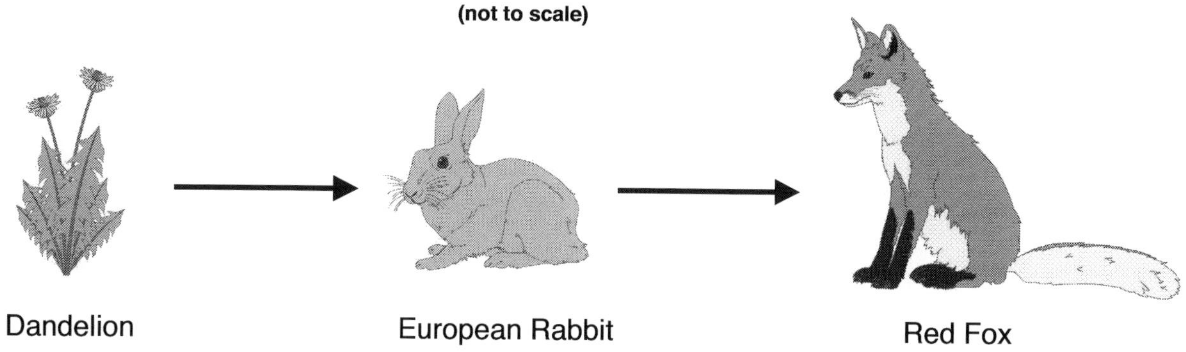

Dandelion   European Rabbit   Red Fox

2 . 1   Explain why plants such as dandelion are important in food chains

3 marks

_____

_____

_____

_____

2 . 2   Ecosystems contain a range of biotic and abiotic factors.

Tick the boxes which show biotic factors.

3 marks

Tick **three** boxes only.

Temperature   ☐

New pathogens   ☐

Oxygen levels   ☐

New predators   ☐

Competition for resources   ☐

A student wanted to find out whether the number of dandelions changed from one side of the school field to the other.

She made the following hypothesis:

Moving away from the woods, the number of dandelions per square metre will increase

Figure 3 shows the school field.

Figure 3

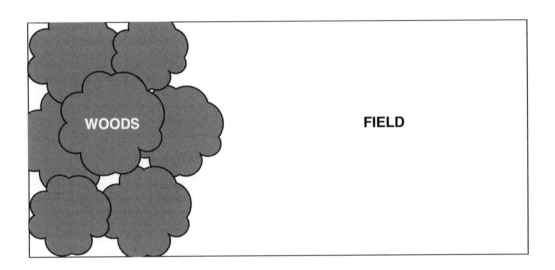

2 . 3   Describe how the student could carry out this investigation.

6 marks

_____

_____

_____

_____

_____

_____

_____

_____

_____

Total = 1

3   If a human touches a hot object, they rapidly pull their hand away.

Figure 4 shows the structures involved in this reflex.

Figure 4

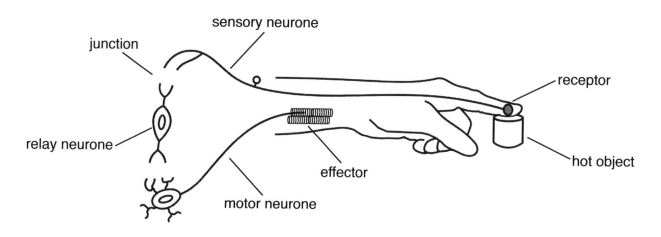

3 . 1   Which of the following shows the correct pathway that information is passed along the reflex arc?

1 mark

Tick **one** box.

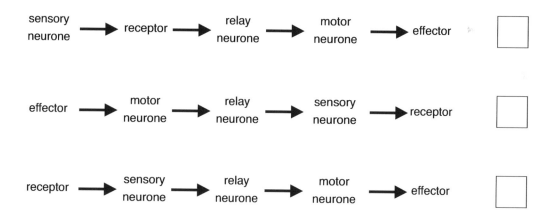

3 . 2   Explain why this is an example of a reflex.

1 mark

_____

_____

_____

3 . 3   In a reflex, the effector brings about the response.

State the type of tissue which forms the effector shown in **figure 4**.

1 mark

_____

3 . 4   Describe what takes place at the junction shown in **figure 4**.

2 marks

_____

_____

_____

3 . 5   The central nervous system (CNS) is an important part of the nervous system.

State the two parts of the central nervous system.

2 marks

_____

_____

3 . 6   Which of the neurones in **figure 4** are found in the central nervous system?

1 mark

_____

Question 3 continues on the next page

A student measured the reaction time of her classmates using the method below.

- Student B sits upright with their dominant hand over the edge of the desk

- Student A positions the ruler with the zero mark between student B's thumb and index finger

- Student A drops the ruler at a random time

- Student B catches the ruler as quickly as they can

- Student A notes the position of the top of the thumb on the ruler

- Student A determines the reaction time from a table

Table 1 shows the results of the experiment.

Table 1

Student	B	C	D	E	F	G	H
Reaction time in milliseconds	347	392	285	405	256	312	274

3 . 7   Calculate the mean reaction time.

Give your answer to four significant figures.

2 marks

Mean reaction time = _____ milliseconds

3 . 8   Explain why we cannot determine a mode for the above results

1 mark

_____

_____

_____

_____

Total = 11

4 The Arctic Fox is found in the cold conditions of Northern Canada where the ground is covered with dense snow in winter

The Arctic Fox belongs to the Canid family. Unlike every other member of the Canid family, the Arctic Fox has fur on the pads of its feet.

This fur reduces the amount of heat lost through the Arctic Fox's foot pads.

Figure 5 shows the Arctic Fox during winter.

Figure 5

Fur on pads
of feet

4 . 1 Scientists believe that the Arctic Fox developed fur on the pads of their feet as a result of evolution.

Describe how this took place.

5 marks

_____

_____

_____

_____

_____

_____

_____

Scientists have discovered fossils of an extinct species of fox.

It is thought that this species was the ancestor of the modern day Arctic Fox.

4.2   What is a fossil?

3 marks

_____

_____

_____

_____

_____

Table 2 shows the classification of the Arctic Fox.

Table 2

Kingdom	Animalia
Phylum	Chordata
Class	Mammalia
	Carnivora
Family	Canidae
Genus	*Vulpes*
Species	*lagopus*

4.3   State the classification grouping missing from the table.

1 mark

_____

4.4   What is the binomial name of the Arctic Fox?

1 mark

_____

Total = 10

5   Many organisms reproduce by sexual reproduction.

Figure 6 shows cells involved in sexual reproduction in humans.

Figure 6

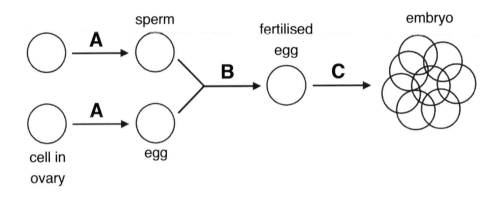

5 . 1   State the part of the body where sperm are produced in humans.

1 mark

_____

5 . 2   State the names of processes A, B and C.

3 marks

         Process A = _____

         Process B = _____

         Process C = _____

5 . 3   Tick the correct boxes in the table below comparing the number of chromosomes in the cells shown.

3 marks

	Half the number of chromosomes	The same number of chromosomes	Twice the number of chromosomes
Compared to a cell in the ovary, an egg cell has ...			
Compared to a sperm cell, a fertilised egg cell has ...			
Compared to a fertilised egg, a cell in the embryo has ...			

5.4   Describe what happens to the cells in an embryo as the embryo develops.

2 marks

_____

_____

_____

5.5   The mass of DNA in a fertilised human egg is 6.6×10^{-12} g.

A fertilised human egg contains 46 chromosomes.

Calculate the average mass of a human chromosome.

Give your answer in standard form to 2 significant figures.

3 marks

Average mass of a human chromosome = _____ g

Total = 12

6　　In mice the colour of the fur pigment is determined by a gene with two alleles.

The allele for black pigment is dominant to the allele for brown pigment.

Figure 7 shows a family tree for a family of mice.

Figure 7

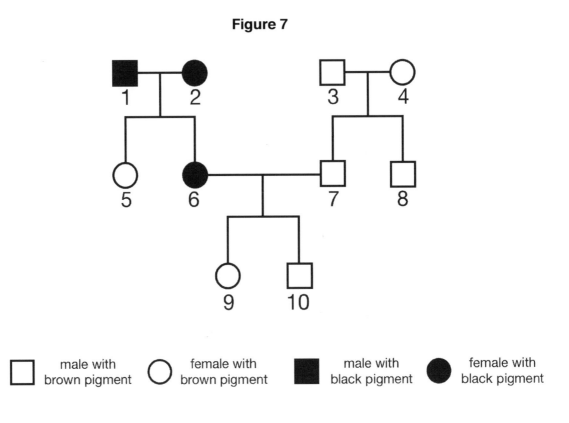

□ male with brown pigment　　○ female with brown pigment　　■ male with black pigment　　● female with black pigment

6 . 1　　Describe how the family tree shows that the allele for brown pigment is recessive.

2 marks

_____

_____

_____

_____

6 . 2   Which pigment alleles are present in mouse 6? Explain your answer.

3 marks

_____

_____

_____

_____

6 . 3   A scientist bred two mice which were both heterozygous for the pigment alleles.

Draw a Punnett square below to show the results of the cross.

In each case, state the genotype and phenotype of the offspring.

Allele for black pigment = B   **Allele for brown pigment = b**

3 marks

6 . 4   The litter produced twelve mice.

Use your cross to predict the number of brown mice in the litter.

Explain your answer.

2 marks

_____

_____

_____

_____

Total = 10

7   The menstrual cycle is controlled by a number of different hormones.

Figure 8 shows how the levels of these hormones vary across the menstrual cycle.

Figure 8

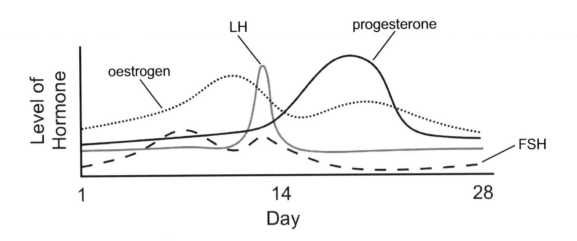

7.1   Describe how the menstrual cycle is controlled by the hormones shown.

6 marks

_____

_____

_____

_____

_____

_____

_____

_____

_____

_____

_____

_____

Total = 6

Printed in Great Britain
by Amazon